Blurtso the Donkey

by Alan Davison

for all things Blurtso, check out his website and blog at:
http://blurtso.com & http://blog.blurtso.com
and his store at: http://www.zazzle.com/blurtsobarn

Shield Publishers
ISBN-13: 978-0986372230
ISBN-10: 0986372234

and...

Harlan the Elephant

Isn't that an odd shape, thought Blurtso, staring at his reflection in the water. That nose, so round and ponderous, like a boxing glove, and that smug little smile, and those attentive, pin-point eyes. What a strange thing it is, that shape, my shape, staring at my shape, that shape. Boxing-glove nose, greyish white, grey body, dark-grey hooves, perked-up ears above attentive eyes. Tuft of hair atop his head. Atop my head. My head housing pin-point eyes looking at his head. Housing looking housing looking. Blurtso one and Blurtso two. Blurtso one and Blurtso too. Double Blurtso smiling smugly, me to me. What does he see when he looks into me? What does he think when he thinks of me? Does he think who on earth could he be? And what's the heart of this mystery?

....

I suppose I should do or say something. A lot of people have subscribed to my blog. I don't want to let them down. But what should I do or say? Maybe I should do something that requires coordination and strength. Like a triple back-flip. That would be impressive! Too bad I don't have coordination and strength. Maybe I should do something funny. Like attempt a triple back-flip without coordination and strength. That might be funny. But it might hurt. I don't like things that hurt. I never have. Before I do anything I ask, "Will this hurt?" It's a good question. Another good question is, "Where's the food?" That may be the best question, because it usually leads to pleasure, unless there isn't any food. Then it's a sad question, perhaps the saddest question of all. Hmmm... I guess I should do or say something. I don't want to let people down.

I wonder if I will like being famous? thought Blurtso. When the world is filled with Blurtso t-shirts and coffee mugs, Blurtso paintings and sculptures and smiling Blurtsos cast in bronze, Blurtso billboards and displays, neon and virtual and Christmas and Easter Blurtsos, and spin-off Blurtsos ad nauseum… I wonder if I will remember these days with nostalgia, when a simple donkey could have a simple meal, and take a nap in the comfort of perfect anonymity.

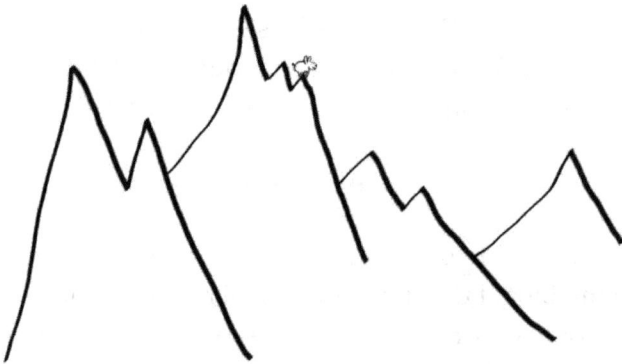

Here I go! said Blurtso, looking down at what lay below. Here I go! he said again, still looking at all the things that lay below. Blurtso's boney little hooves clung tightly to the rocky spine on which he stood, and his pin-point eyes were bright and full of frenzy. Here I go! he said a little more quietly, and with much less conviction. Here I go! Here I go! Here I go! he repeated, and clung even more tightly to the spine that began to cut into his hooves and make them bleed. Here I go! he said more loudly, but with no conviction at all. Here… I… and off he went, slipping, sliding, and tumbling into the only future that awaited him.

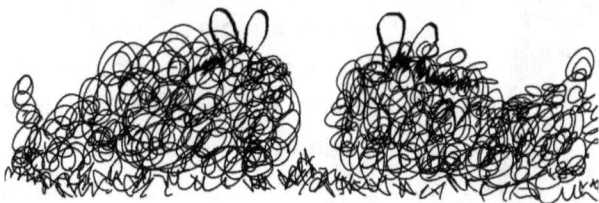

And down the road he went, clippety clopping, stamping, stomping, tramping, tromping, and kicking up dust as he went. Hi ho, sighed Blurtso, putting one hoof in front of the other and thinking of nothing at all. Mile after mile, day after day, year after year, kicking up dust and thinking of nothing at all. What's that? thought Blurtso, noticing a cloud of dust in the distance. It looks like a cloud of dust, he said, kicking up his own dust behind him. Little by little, slowly but surely, hoof after hoof, the two clouds grew nearer. And nearer and nearer, and nearer and nearer, until the two clouds could move no nearer. Hmm, thought Blurtso, peering into the dust that was beginning to settle. What shape is that shape, peering at this shape, peering at me? Boxing glove nose, attentive eyes, dusty little hooves, with a tuft of hair between perked up ears. Hello, said a voice from the dust, I'm Pablo. "Pablo," echoed Blurtso, I'm Blurtso. Your hooves are grey and mine are brown, said Pablo. Your body is brown, and mine is grey, said Blurtso. Hmmm, said Pablo. Hmmm, said Blurtso. The road is quite dusty, said Pablo and Blurtso in unison. Would you like to join me? said Blurtso. I'd love to, said Pablo. And as they started down the road, the dust that was two clouds became one, larger than a single cloud alone.

Mmmm, said Blurtso, taking the first bite of the pumpkin pie he was eating and thinking of all the pumpkin pies he had ever eaten. Mmmm, said Blurtso, taking the second bite of the pumpkin pie he was eating and thinking of all the pumpkin pies he had wanted to eat. Mmmm, said Blurtso, taking the third bite of the pumpkin pie he was eating and thinking of the all the pumpkin pies he was going to eat. Mmmm, said Blurtso, taking the last bite of the pumpkin pie he was eating and wondering where his pumpkin pie had gone while he was eating.

O.k., said the boss, "Pablo the Gardener," what experience do you have? Experience? said Pablo. Yes, said the boss. I'm a gardener, said Pablo. O.k., said the boss, but what can you do? I can make things grow, said Pablo. Very well, said the boss, but can you do anything important? Important? said Pablo. What is more important than making things grow?

I wonder if I'm going the right direction? thought Blurtso, walking across the field. I wonder if I'm making progress? If the world is round, the direction forward is also the direction back. And vice versa. Hmmm, I wonder who invented the idea of progress?

6

The future, thought Blurtso, doing his best to understand the idea. What could that be? Something that has not happened and is not happening and may not happen but will happen in a present that is not this present. Hmm, a present that is not this present. Where does this present end and the next present begin? If I found that point, would that be the future? Blurtso did not have a very big brain, but even he knew that such a point would never be found. There is only one present, he said with confidence, even I know that.

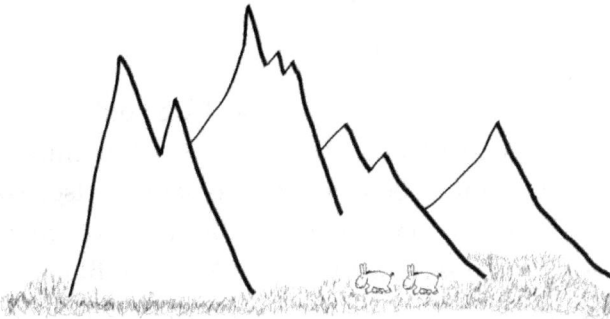

Look at that mountain, said Blurtso, mountains can be exciting! Yes, they can, said Pablo. From the top of that mountain you can see the whole valley! said Blurtso. Yes, said Pablo, but you can't see the mountain.

I'd better make sure everything I use is recyclable, thought Blurtso. Let's see... I use my eyes and my ears and my nose and my hooves, and I sometimes even use my tail. Yep, said Blurtso, I'm completely recyclable.

Happiness, thought Blurtso, sitting with his boxing-glove nose supported on his front left hoof. I see the others, he thought, moving here and there, sniffing and peering, obeying and straying, leading and following with a need on the pillow, a need that stirs them in the morning and settles them in the night. And somehow the reward emerges, from the silence and babble, from above or below, a series of notes rising, repeating in the sound of hoof after hoof after hoof.

Hello, said the devil. Hello, said Blurtso. I see you've come to buy a trombone, said the devil. Have I? said Blurtso. You must have, said the devil. I don't think I need a trombone, said Blurtso. You don't? said the devil. I already have two, said Blurtso. Two trombones! said the devil, you must be very happy! Yes, said Blurtso, I am. Do you want to give me one of your trombones? asked the devil. Absolutely not, said Blurtso. You are happier with two trombones instead of one? said the devil. Yes, said Blurtso, I'm quite fond of my trombones. Well, said the devil, if you are happier with two instead of one, it stands to reason that you would be happier with three instead of two. Yes, said Blurtso, that stands to reason. And if three makes you happier than two, four would make you happier than three. Four trombones? said Blurtso. Absolutely, said the devil, and five and six. I'm not sure, said Blurtso, there must be a point of diminishing trombones. Diminishing trombones? said the devil. When more becomes less, said Blurtso. More becomes less? said the devil, that makes no sense. I suppose it doesn't, said Blurtso, admiring a trombone out of the corner of his eye.

A lot of people seem frustrated.
They seem to think the world, or someone,
owes them something. I don't understand that.
I feel lucky just to be here.

Yes, that's how it is, thought Blurtso, walking a mile in his hooves. That's how it is and I know that's how it is, he said walking, the only way he could walk, in his hooves. I might pretend to know your hooves and you mine, one hoof after another, after all, until we fall, you in yours and me in mine.

Hmm, said Blurtso, licking his hoof and turning the page of the morning paper. Let's see who did what when and why... love hate, give take, future past, slow fast, here there, then now, what when, who how, win lose, live die, settle choose, where why, fortune fame, pardon blame, smoke choke, weep joke, his hers, yours mine, rain shine, sad fine... rolls are fresh and the coffee's free, la dee da dee da dee dee.

"Blurtso sings the donkey electric"

I sing the donkey electric!
A song of asses I sing, near and far!
Asses on hills, asses in fields, asses in herds,
more bountiful than the once-bountiful buffalo,
asses on land and asses at sea, asses short, skinny, fat and tall!
Multitudes of asses,
spanning these star-spangled states!

I have perceived that to be an ass
is to be enough.

The ears of the ass are sacred, delicate,
twitching receptacles of sound,
assiduous antennae registering, recording all,
the hooves of the ass are no less
than the slippers of sultans
striding silken alfombras and seraglio stone,
the snout of the ass and his nostrils—a dual lamp
of Aladdin—inhaling flowery fragrance,
leading to wished-for fiestas of pumpkin pleasure,
the ass's tail, though stumpy or small, and swatting flies,
is a palm fanning reclining Cleopatra,
his teeth, precious jade, are greened and polished
by the grass of a thousand fields,
his attentive eyes and friendly balance of features,
—courtly countenance and caryatid composure—
no less perfect than the visage of Helen.

Such asses I see, to the north and to the south!
From blistering bivouacs of winter
to blazing battalions of summer,
Patagonia to Peloponnese, Malibu to Manhattan,
Concord to Cambridge, every here
and every there, asses I see! Brown, grey,
yellow, red, purple, orange, azure asses!

Asses in other climes, asses in other times,
French, British, Australian, Arabian, Asian asses!

Eating every blade of grass, an ass!
Trampling every leaf that falls, a hoof!
Wading every stream that sings,
a snout, a snort, and a bray!
Hee-haw goes the jack!
Hee-haw goes the jenny!
Hee-haw go the judge and jury and judged!
Hee-haw from the dell! Hee-haw from the glen!
Hee-haw at mid-day! Hee-haw at the moon!

I see the resigned ass, bearing a load,
obeying the coax of his lord,
I see the boisterous ass braying,
in the barn, his bonny bray,
I see the amorous ass (of these there are many),
expressing exigencies by day and by night,
I see farms, fields, freeways and burgs,
each in their way, replete with asininities,
I see the asinine politician, professor, and poet,
each one leaving a brand on the asses of asses.
And the asses of yore, you ask, where are they
with their clip and clop on the stones of the street?
Les ânes voici! I say! Les ânes voici!
Heeding the whinny and neigh,
and ass-bray of the future!

What song do I sing? (you ask and I reply),
I sing the song of asses!
Certain, and stoic, and strong!
From each face an ass!
From each office, family, and farm!
Asses I sing! Avalanches of asses!
I sing! I sing a song of asses!
I sing the donkey electric!

That's far enough, said Blurtso, drawing a line on the ground with the edge of his hoof. The sand was dry and sun-baked and he had to scrape the surface several times before the mark was visible. That's far enough, he repeated, and the others remained on their side of the line. Blurtso remained on his side as well, looking up at the others then looking down at the ground. The sun that had baked the ground was hot and began to bake Blurtso and continued to bake the ground. One by one the others walked away. Then there was only Blurtso, the sun, and the ground... Ooops, said Blurtso, as he let his hoof slip across the line he had drawn in the sand. Ooops, he said, as another hoof crossed, followed by his haunches, his rump, and his stumpy little tail. Ooops, he said, turning and sweeping the line with his boxing-glove nose, then stamping and stomping and tromping until there was no mark left at all. Very good, thought Blurtso, as he surveyed his work and considered his new-found freedom. Freedom? he thought, looking in the direction where the others had gone. Wait for me! he cried, scampering off to join them.

What a lovely day, thought Blurtso, skipping across the field. Excuse me, said a voice, but you'll have to carry a load if you want to continue. As you wish, said Blurtso, bending to accept his load and walking across the field. I'm sorry, said the voice, but you'll have to carry another. And so I shall, said Blurtso, crouching to accept his load and trudging across the field. And another, said the voice. If I must, said Blurtso, kneeling to accept his load and crawling across the field. And another, said the voice. Whew! thought Blurtso, when he could no longer see the day or the field or himself. I hope everything is still waiting, when I'm free of this load that has become myself.

12

O.K., thought Blurtso, I'd better get
serious and do some living. Tell my
friends and tell my family, be engaged
and be engaging, be connected and
accepted, broadcast every thing I'm
thinking, what I am and what I'm not,
what I shall and I shall not, not forgotten when I'm talking, when
I'm sitting, when I'm walking, just as long as I keep talking, are
you listening, are you listening??!!

Hello, said Harlan. Hello, said
Blurtso. Are you waiting for
the bus? No, said Harlan, I'm
going to the river. The river?
said Blurtso. Yes, said Harlan,
to watch the ducks.

The ducks are in fine form, said Blurtso.
Yes, said Harlan, very fine.

What are you thinking about? said Blurtso. I'm thinking about Henry David Thoreau, said Harlan. What about him? said Blurtso. He said it takes infinite leisure to appreciate a single phenomenon. Really? said Blurtso. Yes, said Harlan. In that case, said Blurtso, it's good we had a big lunch.

There goes another snowflake, said Blurtso. I like to watch things that fall—leaves, feathers, snowflakes—things just a little heavier than air. There's something relaxing in watching them let go, something soothing in their acceptance and lack of direction, their trust in the cycle... of soil and stars.

I wonder what I should be when I grow up? I can't be a student for-ever. Unless I go to grad school. But grad students look terrible. They have rings under their eyes like they've been living in a cave. I guess they're worried about their grades. And when they graduate they worry about getting a job. And when they get a job they worry about getting promoted. And when they get promoted they worry about retirement. All because they can't eat grass.

14

Can you teach me to do tai chi? said Blurtso.
Sure, said Harlan, we can begin with a simple
circling exercise.

More slowly, said Harlan, and a little less
like an airplane propeller.

Circle from side to side, said Blurtso,
shifting your weight from hoof to hoof…
left hoof full, right hoof empty,
right hoof full, left hoof empty,
see the pumpkin pie, see the empty pie tin…

They say dogs bark when they see a spirit, and they can sense when a person has died. But I've never seen a spirit, even when I was standing next to a barking dog. I wonder what else I'm missing?

The moon is full. They say a full moon brings out the animal in you. I wonder what animal is in me? A bull, or a goat, or a parakeet? I've never really thought about my inner parakeet. I wonder how long it's been trying to get out? I wonder if it's unhealthy to keep it locked up. The world might be a different place, if we all got in touch with our inner parakeets.

What's your inner parakeet telling you? said Harlan. He's telling me, said Blurtso, that there's a half-eaten pumpkin pie in the fridge. What's yours telling you? He's telling me, said Harlan, that some-one already finished the second half.

16

Hmm, thought Blurtso, the ants have returned to the barn. I wonder what they do in winter... I've never seen a colony migrating south. Maybe they go deeper underground. They sure are in a hurry, always going someplace. And as soon as they get there, they go someplace else. They're almost human... I wonder if ants ever sleep? I wonder what they dream of? I wonder if they dream of going here and there and back again? I suppose if you dream of what you do when you're awake, it's like you've never been asleep... Ants don't take many naps. I've never seen an ant napping under a tree. Whenever I'm under a tree, the ants that are there crawl all over me. I wouldn't mind napping with an ant, but I'm not sure they're capable. The ability to nap is an uncommon skill... I wonder if ants worry about the environment? I wonder what they think of global warming? If I were an ant I would want to do something, but they act like they don't even care. Maybe they don't take themselves as seriously as we do. Maybe for them this world is just a testing ground, and they'll all get their reward in heaven. I wonder what an ant has to do to get into heaven? I wonder what heaven is for an ant? Maybe it's a warm barn with plenty of food. That's what it is for me. And since a warm barn with plenty of food always has a number of ants, and usually a donkey or two, then I must be a part of their heaven and they must be a part of mine. Maybe heaven is not a place at all... maybe it's a relationship.

Isn't it amazing, said Blurtso, how people can spend so much time building something, then never look at it when they're done? What do you mean? said Harlan. This tree house, said Blurtso. Alex and I built it almost two years ago, and when we were building it we selected the boards with the greatest care, then measured and cut them, nailed and braced them, then raised the pole with the house on top, and then we climbed up and never really looked at it again. What's this nick in the rail? said Harlan. That? That's where I dropped the skill saw when my ice cream fell out of its cone. There's a nail missing here, said Harlan. Yes, said Blurtso, it kept poking out, so I removed it. What are these scratches? That's from my screwdriver, said Blurtso, when I was screwing down the floor boards. And this stain? That's the grape juice I spilled when I was using the nail gun. And this burned spot? That's where I set down the circular sander with the power on. You do beautiful work, said Harlan. Thank you, said Blurtso.

One way to experience a moment completely,
is to try as hard as you can
to experience a moment completely,
until you experience complete frustration.

Harlan? said Blurtso. Yes? said Harlan. Are you awake? Yes, said Harlan. What are you thinking of? Einstein's theory of time, said Harlan. What? said Blurtso. You know, said Harlan, the discovery that time passes more slowly the faster you move. Is that true? said Blurtso. Yes, said Harlan. So I would live longer, said Blurtso, if I moved more quickly? Yes, said Harlan. And if I ran in my sleep, said Blurtso, I would get more sleep?

****

Harlan? said Blurtso. Yes? Are you awake? Yes, said Harlan. What are you thinking about? Mortality, said Harlan. Mortality? said Blurtso. Yes, said Harlan, do you believe in reincarnation? I'm not sure, said Blurtso, what's reincarnation? That's when your soul comes back as a different animal. After you die? said Blurtso. Yes, said Harlan, if you live a good life you come back as a higher one, and if you live a bad life you come back as a lower one. A lower animal? said Blurtso. Yes, said Harlan. Like a human? said Blurtso.

****

Harlan? said Blurtso. Yes? said Harlan. Are you awake? Yes, said Harlan. What are you thinking about? said Blurtso. Differences, said Harlan. Differences? said Blurtso. Yes, said Harlan, political, religious, and personal differences. Like what one person thinks is fun and another does not, and what one thinks is proper and another does not, and what one thinks is necessary and another does not. Yes, said Blurtso, it's amazing we ever get along. I suppose, said Harlan, that's what love is for.

19

Hmm, thought Blurtso, number 82. Everywhere I go, someone is always giving me a number. And it's different every time. I'm starting to think they don't know who I am.

I don't think I'm very human, said Blurtso. Why not? said Harlan. I've been watching television all day, said Blurtso, and I haven't seen a single thing I liked. What do you mean? said Harlan. Well, said Blurtso, I'm not interested in owning an automobile, I don't want insurance, I don't eat meat, I don't drink beer, I don't care about celebrities, I'm not in a hurry, and I'd rather play a sport than watch it. Well, said Harlan, that just about covers it. And oh yes, said Blurtso, I have no interest in movies where things are blowing up. You're right, said Harlan, you're not very human. What do you think it would be like, said Harlan, if there were more donkeys on TV? I don't really know, said Blurtso, I guess there would be a lot more wandering around… sort of like a golf tournament without balls and clubs.

Hmm… it sure is nice to swing back and forth… and synchronize your breath to the motion… inhale forward, exhale back, inhale forward, exhale back… Hmmm… I'm really soaring… wow, I guess it's as close as I'll get to flying… unless I go parasailing… like Pablo in Mexico… Pablo doesn't have a timid bone in his body… maybe I should write a famous novel and make Pablo the hero… but then my novel would be fact instead of fiction… and I already have enough facts in my life… like the fact I'm late for school… Hmmm… it sure is relaxing… to synchronize your breath… I wonder if the birds synchronize their breath to the beat of their wings… it would be nice to be able to fly, but I wouldn't want to be a bird… wings are even clumsier than hooves… especially for cell phones and texting… I don't think I've ever seen a bird texting… no matter how nervous he was… and birds are very nervous… I guess I would be too, if I were smaller than a cat… but I'm bigger than cats… and that simplifies things… like swinging… back and forth… and in and out… I wonder if my class is over… I wonder if I missed the final… I think today was the last day… Hmmm… it sure is relaxing… to swing back and forth… and breathe in and out… I'll bet I could swing all day… if I didn't get hungry… I'll bet I could just keep on swinging… back and forth, and in and out… marking my path… as effortlessly as… the path… of a planet.

I admire grass, thought Blurtso. It never gets discouraged. It keeps on growing no matter how often they mow it down. And in a storm it just bends in the wind. It makes me happy to think... we are what we eat.

Hmm, the grass is equally green.

It's easy to identify problems from up here, but impossible to do anything.

I thought this would be more comfortable.

Look at the people on both sides working furiously to fortify the fence, as if life depended on it.

I'm several feet off the ground, but I don't feel courageous.

Harlan was talking a lot about mindfulness yesterday. I wonder what he meant? I wonder if it's anything like stomachfulness? I'll have to ask him the next time I see him, if I'm not too focused on the present to remember.

An individual blade of grass is inconceivable. It only exists as the pattern of relationships—seed, soil, roots, water, sun—called grass. An individual donkey is also inconceivable.

If a single blade of grass exists only as a part of the pattern called grass, and the pattern called grass exists only as a part of the pattern called the world, and the pattern called the world exists only as a part of the pattern called the universe, then everything that exists exists only as pattern, and it is impossible to speak of grass, or pumpkin pies, or "Blurtso", without speaking of the universe.

Hmm… it's starting to rain. I wonder if I should go into a shop. If I do I'll probably miss my bus, and then I'll have to wait for the next one. And if it keeps raining I'll miss that one and have to wait for the next one, and the next one… hmm... and then it'll get dark, and the shop will close, and they'll throw me out after the last bus leaves, and I'll have to spend the night in the rain, and in the dark… hmm... unless I hitch-hike, but no one will stop for a wet donkey, unless someone does, someone who has bad intentions, or owns a forced-labor copper mine... and I'll be donkey-napped and flown to the mine on a private jet smuggling military secrets, and I'll be forced to work night and day, living on coca leaves and betel nut, knowing that the future of the world lays in my hooves, if I can only escape and steal back the secrets... and I'll have to bribe the guards, and slip into the hills and build a raft... and sail it to the sea where I'll board a steamer... and I'll cross the Atlantic, until the ship hits an ice burg and sinks... and I'll climb into a lifeboat which I'll sail through the wreckage pulling out survivors... and they'll all be grateful, all but the one who is a guard from the mine and has been following me, and is going to kill me the minute we reach Greenland…

Hey, it stopped raining!

O.k., said Blurtso, on three. One, two, three... Go!
And off they went as fast as they could.
Hmm, thought Blurtso, Pavlov was right.

Goodness me! thought Blurtso. Look at all these runners and bikes!
Maybe I should do a marathon, or triathlon, or decathlon....
If I trained night and day,
I'm sure I could beat myself at something.

I love the smell of wood in autumn, and the sound of dry leaves. This is a very nice log. I wonder which tree it came from? I suppose it was like any other tree, growing slowly, drinking minerals, seeking sun. I suppose birds built nests in its branches, and squirrels chased up and down. I suppose it was at the center of a universe of sights and sounds, never thinking it would fall, and be hollowed out. I guess the shell always outlasts the heart, and the forest is strewn with empty armor. And every living thing is immortal... until it dies.

Oh no! said Blurtso, I'm going to be fired!
How can I cover my tracks?!
I know, I'll apply for promotion!!

Hey, thought Blurtso, my ears cast a shadow, like the shadow
of a sundial, moving around the lawn... It's a quarter to three.
I guess the poet was right, we *are* made of time.

Occasionally, I free my mind to the day,
I feel the sounds, the colors, the breeze,
and I remember this day, which is every day, a lifetime.

www.ingramcontent.com/pod-product-compliance
Lightning Source LLC
Chambersburg PA
CBHW060606030426
42337CB00019B/3639